Ernst S. Marzell
Great Inventions
Illustrated by Erich Hölle

Published by
Lerner Publications Company
Minneapolis, Minnesota

Contents

First published in the United States 1973 by
Lerner Publications Company,
Minneapolis, Minnesota
All United States and Canadian rights reserved

Published simultaneously in Canada by
J. M. Dent & Sons Ltd, Don Mills,
Ontario

Text and illustrations Copyright ©
1973 Verlag Carl Ueberreuter
English Translation Copyright © 1973
Kaye & Ward Ltd, London, England

First published in Austria as *Die
Grossen Erfindungen* by Verlag
Carl Ueberreuter, Vienna in 1973

ISBN: 0–8225–0705–6
Library of Congress Catalog Card
Number: 75–113420

Printed in Austria and bound in the
United States

Introduction

From the very beginning man has been an inventor. The first inventions were the tools the first men made to make their lives better: knives, spears and arrows to hunt game, axes to cut down wood for shelters, and needles to sew clothes to keep themselves warm.

For a long time invention was a very slow process. Hundreds of thousands of years separate the invention of stone tools, the plow, the wheel, and metal-working. By the Middle Ages invention had speeded up considerably, but even so hundreds of years could pass before knowledge of an invention spread—as happened, for example, with paper-making. With the invention of printing from metal type it became easier for knowledge and ideas to spread and for one inventor to benefit from the discoveries and theories of other men distant from him, both in time and place. Today the Western world has such a rich technical heritage that inventions happen almost too quickly for us to keep up with them.

Great inventions do not often occur simply as sudden flashes of inspiration in the minds of great men. There is usually a long and laborious process of experimentation, of failure, then partial success before a new idea can be made to work. Usually an inventor is building on the discoveries of earlier inventors. Printing, for example, depended on the earlier inventions of paper, of a suitable metal for casting the type, and of suitable printing inks. It also used skills and techniques known to goldsmiths, engravers, and woodcut printers. Sometimes too the same idea is developed by a number of men independently: this happened with the internal combustion engine and the automobile, the jet engine, photography, the screw-propeller and the water turbine.

Here you can read about some of the most important and exciting inventions that have changed, and are changing, the world we live in.

Agriculture

The first men hunted wild animals and gathered berries for food. Then about 10,000 years ago, men began to *grow* food. They collected the seeds of wild plants and sowed them in the ground. Stone-Age peoples discovered and first cultivated cereals that are still staple foods for the world today, including wheats, barleys, rice, millet and maize.

At first they had only digging-sticks to turn the soil with and to make holes for the seeds. Much later, about 3000 BC, the plow was invented in Mesopotamia. This first plow was little more than a forked branch pulled by an ox, but its invention marks the beginning of agriculture.

The idea of using animals for pulling a plow may well have led to the invention of the cart. Until then heavy loads had been dragged or moved over wooden rollers. From these rollers the wheel developed, first as a solid disc with a hole bored in the center—the hub—and fitted on to a crossbar—the axle. The wheel was improved and improved, until at last the spoked wheel was invented.

The farmer's way of life was quite different from the hunter's, for he had to stay in one place to harvest his crops. Men now lived in settlements.

Pottery

Stone-Age men also learned how to fire clay to make pots. In making a pot, the potter was creating something absolutely new: he was turning a substance that became soft in water into a hard substance that could *hold* water. Pots were made entirely by hand until a potter's wheel was invented. On a wheel a pot could be built up quickly, but it needed much skill to use it and so pottery became one of the first specialist crafts.

Iron

Iron is found in the earth as iron ore, which is a chemical compound of iron and oxygen, mixed with impurities such as sand, clay and limestone. Iron ore is of no use until it has been changed into pure iron. By 2500 BC men in the Near East had learned to release the metal from its ore by heating it with charcoal. These men had by chance stumbled on the correct chemical process to smelt iron: for the carbon in charcoal, when heated, starts a chain of chemical reactions which in the end leave the iron in a pure state. Men did not discover *why* this happened until the *twentieth* century.

This first iron was soft and broke easily. Then about 1400 BC the Hittites learned that iron would become hard if it was hammered while hot: they had learnt to *forge* it.

In 900 BC blacksmiths discovered that by heating iron with charcoal and then plunging it in cold water they could make a harder and stronger metal.

Men had already learned to work other metals—gold, silver, tin, lead, copper—and to combine tin and copper to make bronze, but iron was the most important discovery. It was a much stronger metal and so made powerful weapons and stronger tools. It is also one of the commonest elements in the earth, so it was possible for many people to have iron weapons and goods. Before only kings and very important people could afford things made from the other, more precious, metals.

Ships

The first ships were made of logs tied together or from hollowed tree-trunks. They were used to cross rivers and lakes.

The Phoenicians were among the first *sea-going* peoples. As early as 800 BC they sailed to the Gulf of Guinea, England and even India. They had sailing ships and rowing galleys. The sailing ship had a single mast and a square sail attached to a crossbeam. The galley also had a mast and sail, but it was really a rowing ship: it had two, sometimes three, banks of oars. The sailing ship was used by traders; the galley was a warship and rowed by slaves.

Over the centuries ships developed slowly. The first steering oar became a paddle-shaped rudder worked by a tiller; more masts and sail were added—to make the typical galleon of the 16th century. These square-sailed ships could only sail with the wind. A jib—a triangular sail making it possible to sail *against* the wind—was not used until the 18th century, although the Arabs had introduced it to Europe hundreds of years earlier. Not until the plane was invented did men realize *why* the jib worked.

In the 19th century iron ships driven by steam engines replaced sailing ships; then turbine-ships replaced steam-ships. Now some ships are driven by nuclear energy.

The first steamships had paddles, but in 1826 an Austrian, Josef Ressel, invented the screw-propeller. As a screwdriver drives a screw deeper into the wood with each turn, so the ship's engine turns the screw propelling the ship forward through the water. The screw increased speeds and saved fuel.

Ships are still today a vital part of world trade.

The Mariner's Compass

The mariner's compass is a magnetized needle freely balanced on a pivot. Wherever it is, it will always swing to the magnetic North. It works because it is acted upon by the earth's magnetism, for the earth itself acts as a magnet with ends at the magnetic North and South Poles.

Until the invention of the compass, ships had to steer by the sun and stars. The compass made ocean navigation possible and opened up the world.

It is not known who invented the compass. It probably developed from the lodestone, magnetic iron ore which occurs naturally in the earth. Greek, Chinese, Arab and Italian sailors used the lodestone to help them navigate; the Vikings used it when they sailed to America in the 10th century AD.

By the 12th century the compass was known in Europe and the Italians in particular made improvements to the early versions.

Today ships use the gyro compass, which depends on the spin of the earth for its action; unlike the magnetic compass, its readings are not affected by steel hulls. But all ships must carry magnetic compasses and they are still used to land aircraft.

Machines

The first machine invented was the lever, which made it possible for men to lift and move weights too heavy to be raised unaided. The lever is still an essential part of many modern—and very much more complex—machines.

The pulley is also an early invention. It is a combination of a grooved wheel or wheels and ropes.

The Greeks were the first to understand the principles of mechanical power. In the 3rd century BC Archimedes developed the lever and the screw. He made machines from pulleys and winches which were used in ship-building, and he also made engines of war to catapult stones.

The first mechanical clock was made by the Chinese in the 8th century AD. It was driven by a weight and balance: the suspended beam balance was pushed one way and then the other by a weight attached to a toothed wheel. This escapement mechanism makes it possible to run a machine at a constant speed. Time could now be accurately measured.

Mechanical clocks reached Europe in the 13th century. One of the earliest still surviving is in England at Salisbury Cathedral. It was made in 1386.

Paper

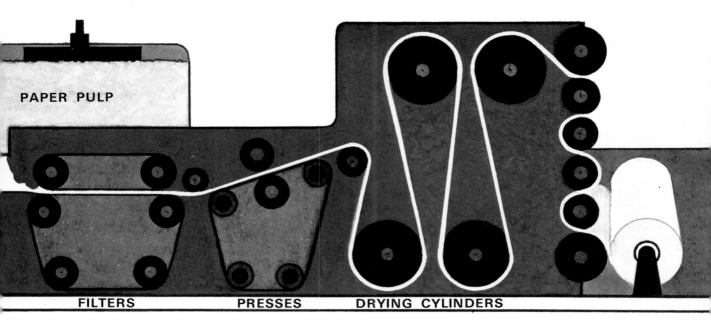

PAPER PULP

FILTERS   **PRESSES**   **DRYING CYLINDERS**

PAPYRUS

The Chinese learned to make paper in the 2nd century AD. They made a pulp by crushing and soaking tree bark, rags and old fishing nets in water, then spread it out thinly to dry in the sun. As the pulp dried the fibers knitted together into paper. Later, the Chinese made a mold, which was dipped into the pulp and as the water drained off a smoother sheet of paper formed.

The Arabs learned the art from Chinese prisoners and introduced it into Europe in the 12th century. Paper was made by hand until a Frenchman, Louis Robert, invented a machine in 1799. In a paper machine the pulp travels along a moving belt of wire mesh, through which the water drains, leaving the fibers on top; then presses squeeze the fibers into a smooth, wet sheet which is passed between felt mats and hot cylinders until it is dry.

Today, paper is made from cellulose, wood and plant fibers and old paper; rags make strong paper, but are expensive, so they are used only for bank notes and legal documents.

Without paper, printing would not have been possible. Earlier writing materials, such as clay, wax, stone and parchment, were quite unsuitable; and although paper gets its name from papyrus, this was too hard and brittle for printing on. Without a paper-making machine, the paper industry could not have provided enough paper for the mass production of newspapers and books. Papermaking is one of the biggest modern industries.

Printing

In the 15th century, as more and more people could read, the manuscript copiers and woodcut printers could not meet the demand for books. When about 1440 Johann Gutenberg of Mainz invented a method of printing from movable type, it became possible to mass produce books by mechanical means. Gutenberg's invention revolutionized the Western world: it was the first way of mass communication—of knowledge and ideas—between men.

Gutenberg cast letters in metal from molds and with them "composed" the book. He made a press to print identical copies of the same book. Afterwards he could use the type again to compose another book.

Gutenberg's method of printing is called *letterpress*. The printing ink touches only the surface of the raised letters and the press transfers their images to paper. It is still an important process today, although it is now highly mechanized: machines cast and assemble the type in the correct order, where once it was done by hand; the letters are not used again but are melted down for recasting.

The other major printing process is *lithography*, which was invented by Aloys Senefelder in 1798. This works on the principle that grease rejects water: the flat printing surface is prepared with water so that only the greased image to be printed picks up the ink. By lithography, photographs and full color pictures can be printed in the same way and on the same page as the type.

All printing presses were flat-bed machines moving to-and-fro until the invention of the rotary press; this revolving cylinder is the fastest printing process today and is used particularly for newspapers which are printed on a con-

Johann Gutenberg, 1400–68

tinuous web of paper fed from a roll.

From the Lens to the Telescope

Galileo Galilei, 1564–1642

In 1608 a Dutch spectacle-maker accidentally put two lenses together and made a telescope. Galileo, the great Italian scientist, improved the focus of the lenses to such an extent that he was able to see hills and valleys on the moon. The telescope was an important discovery for it helped men realize the smallness of the earth and the immensity of the universe.

In Galileo's telescope the object glass was a convex lens and the eyepiece a concave lens. Kepler showed that it could be further improved with a convex eyepiece; with such a telescope Huygens discovered a moon of Saturn in 1655. These *refracting* telescopes became longer and longer to increase magnification (some were 210 ft.) and were too unwieldy for practical use. Then in 1668 Isaac Newton invented the *reflecting* telescope which used two mirrors to reflect the image onto the magnifying lens. The mirrors improved the focus of the telescope. This telescope was of a practicable size.

Many more improvements have been made to the telescope. The largest reflector telescope today is at Mount Palomar Observatory in California and has a 200-in. lens. These modern giant telescopes are huge film cameras which can record what the eye cannot see. With them it is possible to photograph heavenly bodies thousands of light-years away.

Steam Engines

The Newcomen engine, named after its English inventor, was the first engine to be worked by steam driving forward a piston in a cylinder. It was used to pump water out of mines, but it was clumsy, wasteful of fuel and not easy to adapt for other purposes.

In 1765, while repairing a Newcomen engine, James Watt, a Scottish instrument maker, solved the problem of steam wastage caused by the cylinder having to be alternately cooled and reheated: he made a separate condenser. Watt had invented the first steam engine of practical use.

Watt improved his engine by the invention of "parallel motion", making his piston *pull* as well as push. When he succeeded in making it drive a revolving shaft, it could be adapted to drive machinery of all kinds, and in 1785 steam engines were used in mills to work looms.

Steam engines could now be used to drive ships: Robert Fulton's *Clermont*, a paddle-driven steamship operating on the Hudson River, was the first commercially successful one; in 1807 it traveled the 150 miles from New York to Albany in 30 hours.

The steam engine created a new form of transport—railway locomotives. Railways had been in use for some time, but operated by horses. They were run on a small scale between mine or mill and canal or port. George Stephenson, an English engineer, made the first loco-motive to pull wagons of coal from mine to port; he saw that it could be used to provide public transport for people and goods, and in 1825 his engine successfully pulled the first public passenger train on the Stockton to Darlington Railway in England. This was a very important invention for industry, for goods and raw materials could now be moved quickly, cheaply and in great quantities.

Today the piston engine has largely been replaced by the steam turbine, in which a jet of steam is forced against a revolving disc with curved blades around its edge. The turbine is smoother, more efficient and more powerful.

James Watt, 1736–1819　　　*Robert Fulton, 1765–1815*

Electricity

The discovery of the Danish scientist Oersted that there is a link between magnetism and electricity led to Michael Faraday's discovery in 1831 that an electric current could be induced in a coil of wire by moving a magnet through it. Alexander Volta had already made a battery which had produced the first continuous and controllable electric current from a chemical solution: but Faraday's discovery made it possible to generate the large and powerful currents that we use today. The magnet and coil is still the basic principle of the modern generator.

Modern generators are

Michael Faraday,
1791–1867

Thomas Alva Edison,
1847–1931

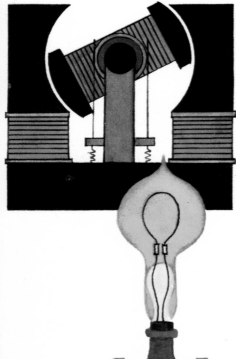

driven by steam and water turbines. The current is then carried long distances by high tension cables to wherever it is needed.

The first generators produced only a little electricity, but there was little demand even for this. It was used mainly for electroplating (putting a thin coat of metal on articles made from other metals) and for carbon-arc lamps. Humphry Davy had discovered that when two carbon rods, connected to an electric battery, were touched together and then slightly separated, a flame—or arc— of brilliant light was produced. The electric arc was later used for welding, flood and search lights and movie projectors, but it was not a satisfactory source of ordinary lighting and was little used. The first real demand for electricity came with the invention of the light bulb.

Thomas Edison's light bulb was made from a piece of thin carbon enclosed in an airless glass tube; when an electric current was passed through this filament, it glowed with heat. Edison built the first power station in New York in 1882 to supply electricity to people using his lamps. Soon public power stations were built to meet the increasing demand for electricity as more and more uses were found for it. Today we use electricity to run machines in factories and in the home, to drive trains, and to provide light and heat.

Chemistry

Chemistry is the study of materials: how they are made up from over a hundred elements and how they can be changed. From the work of chemists developed the industrial chemical industry.

In 1840 Liebig showed that plants take in carbon and oxygen from the air, hydrogen and oxygen from water, and nitrates and other compounds from the soil. He also showed that growing crops exhausts the soil's natural supply of nitrates and other substances. This discovery led to the manufacture of chemical fertilizers to put these sub-stances back artificially into the soil.

Chemists succeeded in making a wide variety of sub-stances: for example, sodium compounds which are used in different forms in the soap, paper, glass and textile indus-tries, as a bleach and as an essential part of our diet (salt). These substances separately have a wide application: sul-furic acid, for example, is used to make fertilizers, dyes, rayon, explosives and in other chemical industries. From the chemical dye industry, which began with William Perkin making a mauve dye from

Justus von Liebig, 1803–73

coal tar in 1856, developed paints, drugs, weed-killers and insecticides.

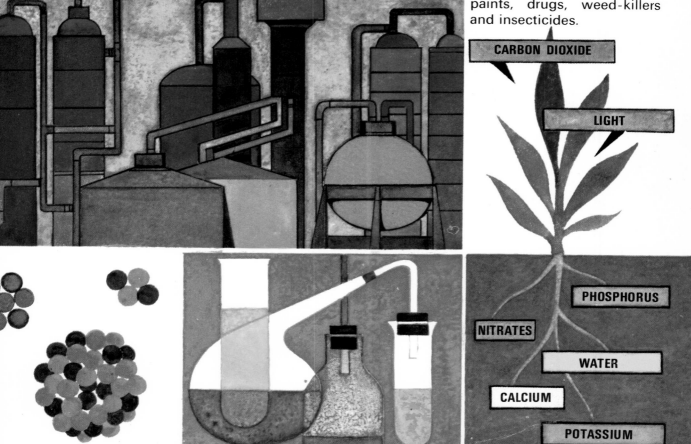

CARBON DIOXIDE

LIGHT

PHOSPHORUS

NITRATES

WATER

CALCIUM

POTASSIUM

Photography

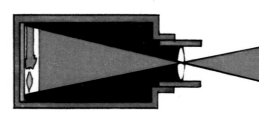

William Henry Fox Talbot, 1800–77

The camera developed from the camera obscura. This was a darkened box with a small hole at one end. When light entered through the hole an image of the object or scene outside was thrown onto the opposite inner wall. In 1837 Daguerre, a Frenchman, first made this image permanent; he made a photograph by the action of light on an iodized silver plate in a camera. Although the daguerreotype became a popular process, particularly in America, the important invention for the subsequent development of photography was Fox Talbot's negative-positive process, using a chemically prepared paper. By this process many true prints, or positives, could be made from the negative, whereas copies of the daguerreotype could only be made by copying the original picture.

George Eastman marketed the first portable camera, the No. 1 Kodak, in 1888. This used roll film. The camera itself had to be returned to the manufacturer to develop the film and reload the camera.

The first photographs which could be run consecutively as a film (48 images a second) were taken by Thomas Edison in 1889 of a galloping horse. In 1895 Louis and Auguste Lumière built a machine, the Cinématographe, for projecting pictures.

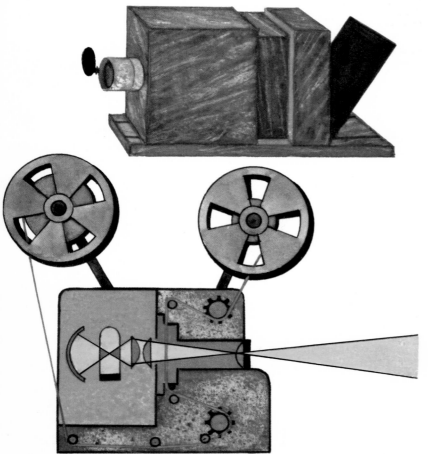

Raw Materials

Henry Bessemer, 1813–98

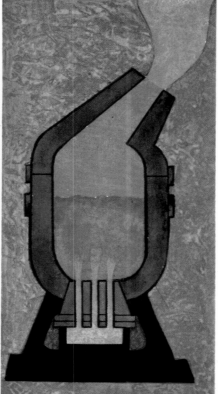

NATURAL GAS

MINERAL OIL

In 1856 Henry Bessemer, an Englishman, made a modern blast furnace capable of making high quality steel very quickly and in large quantities. He replaced the open furnace with a container with a small hole at the top. He filled it with molten iron and forced blasts of air through at great pressure. The oxygen in the air combined with the carbon in the iron to produce great heat and carry away all the impurities as gas, leaving mild steel behind. This process was a key factor in the success of the Industrial Revolution.

*

Thousands of feet below the earth's surface lie vast fields of mineral oil. In 1859 the first "well" to extract this oil was bored in Pennsylvania; this was the beginning of the modern oil-refining industry.

Today oil is an indispensible part of modern industry and modern life. It provides fuel for all kinds of land, sea and air transport and for industrial and domestic heating. The by-products of the industry are used in the manufacture of synthetic rubber, plastics, machine lubricants, detergents, anaesthetics, printing inks, nylon, vaseline, paraffin, asphalt and countless other chemical products.

18

Explosives

Alfred Bernhard Nobel, 1833–96

Gunpowder, the first explosive, was invented in China about two thousand years ago. It is made of saltpeter, carbon and sulfur. The Chinese used it at first for fireworks and later for warfare.

The Arabs introduced gunpowder to Europe, where it was used for cannons, siege-engines and firearms. It was also used in mining and quarrying, its blasting power achieving what had before required brute force.

Gunpowder is dangerous to use because it is hard to control, but it is not very powerful. For many of the civil-engineering projects of the 19th century—tunnelling for example—it was not effective. It is therefore little used today, except in blasting when a "slow" push is needed to prevent excessive break-up.

Experiments with nitro-glycerine, which is made by the action of nitric and sulfuric acids on glycerine, showed that it had tremendous explosive energy. But because it was highly flammable, people were reluctant to use it for practical purposes. Then in 1867 a Swede, Alfred Nobel, succeeded in combining nitro-glycerine with kieselguhr, which reduced its flammability to such an extent that the explosion could be controlled. He had made dynamite.

Gelignite and TNT were subsequently made from nitrogen, but dynamite was the first really powerful explosive. The most powerful today are nuclear explosives.

The Internal Combustion Engine

Gottlieb Daimler, 1834–1900

Henry Ford, 1863–1947

An *internal* combustion engine is so called because the fuel is burnt in the engine, not in a separate boiler. Fuel is put into the cylinder, compressed by a piston and ignited: this explosion pushes the piston back turning the engine shaft. Then the piston expels the burnt gases so the process can be repeated.

Nikolaus Otto, a German engineer, built the first internal combustion engine in 1876, but it ran at a very low speed. Gottlieb Daimler, who worked for Otto, patented a successful high-speed internal combustion engine in 1885; he used gasoline as fuel (Otto had used gas) and an electric spark for the ignition.

The gasoline engine powered the first successful automobile and is still the most suitable engine for this purpose. But the automobile was little more than an expensive toy until an American, Henry Ford, began to mass produce them cheaply in 1908. Ford saw the usefulness of the automobile and made it the necessity that it is today.

The gasoline engine was also the only engine light enough (in weight) to power the first planes.

The other major kind of internal combustion engine today is the diesel, named after its inventor. In the diesel no ignition spark is needed: compression produces the explosion. It burns heavier and cheaper oil, and is used in trains, ships and buses.

Water Power

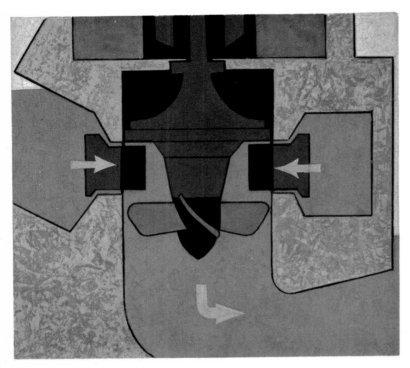

Victor Kaplan, 1876–1934

Water is a very old source of power; it was transformed into modern industrial power by the invention of the water turbine engine.

The waterwheel made use of only a fraction of the water power available, because the pressure of the water was on only *half* the wheel at any one time. In the turbine engine the wheel is placed *horizontally* so that the force of the water will drive *all* the paddles at the *same* time. Victor Kaplan made the turbine even more efficient with blades that could be varied to the correct angle for different flows of water. Today there are different kinds of turbines for different conditions. One of the most modern turbines is the Deriaz, named after its inventor; it is in use at Niagara Falls, Canada.

The most important use of water turbines is as generators of electricity. Hydro-generators provide electricity more cheaply than steam, coal or oil.

Hydro-electric plants can use tidal waters, waterfalls, and water from rivers, lakes and artificial reservoirs. Because their "raw material" involves no heavy transport costs, hydro-power plants can be built in remote districts, bringing new industry to previously uneconomic areas.

Medicine

*Alexander Fleming,
1881–1955*

The healing—and poisonous—powers of plants have long been known, but not until the 19th century did chemists succeed in identifying and separating the special substances from their crude plant sources. Until then drugs had been made simply by crushing the plant with a pestle in a mortar.

The first drugs to be isolated from their natural plant sources were morphine (relieves pain), quinine (cures malaria), and the poisons strychnine and atropine.

When chemists had discovered how the substances were made, they experimented until they were able to make them artificially from simple chemicals.

At the same time doctors were beginning to realize that many illnesses are caused by *bacteria*—one-celled plants so small they can only be seen under a microscope and present everywhere in air, soil and water. Penicillin, made from a fungus of the Penicillium group, was the first drug found to be effective against a great range of these organisms. It was discovered by chance when an English doctor, Alexander Fleming, noticed in his laboratory that a mold of this particular kind had destroyed bacteria. It took the chemists Florey and Chain ten years to isolate it in large enough quantities and in a pure enough form for it to be used as a drug.

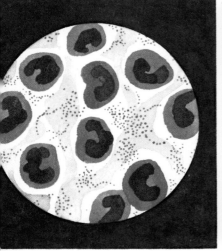

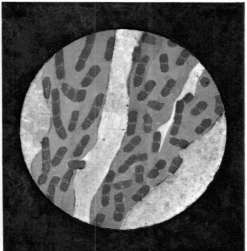

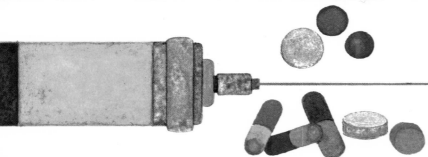

Flight

In 1783 two Frenchmen, the Montgolfier brothers, made a hot-air balloon to carry men up in the air. In 1900 Graf Zeppelin developed the airship from the balloon: this "Zeppelin", which had a rigid framework and was propelled by a gasoline engine, crossed the Atlantic many times.

But the plane—and flight as we know it—did not develop from the balloon, for the two work on completely opposite principles. The balloon is lighter than air and is supported by it; the plane is heavier than air and is held up by the dynamic pressure of air—by the force of air in motion.

Unlike other forms of transport, the plane works as a complete structure. Change one part and the rest of the plane will be affected. A plane with propellers moves through the air in the same way as a ship with a screw through water (page 6); at the same time the pressure developed by motion between the wings and air, as the plane moves, gives the "lift" to keep it up. The tail provides balance and control.

The Wright brothers made the first successful plane. It was very light and flimsy, more like a kite than a modern plane, and it had a petrol engine. In 1903 in North Carolina their plane flew for just twelve seconds— but it was the beginning of flight.

Orville Wright, 1871–1948   *Wilbur Wright, 1867–1912*

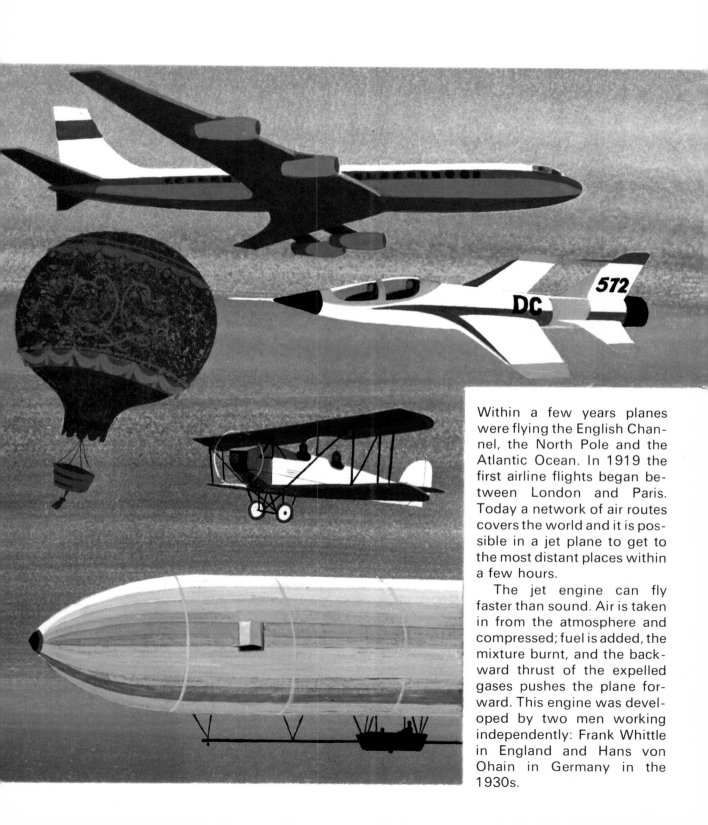

Within a few years planes were flying the English Channel, the North Pole and the Atlantic Ocean. In 1919 the first airline flights began between London and Paris. Today a network of air routes covers the world and it is possible in a jet plane to get to the most distant places within a few hours.

The jet engine can fly faster than sound. Air is taken in from the atmosphere and compressed; fuel is added, the mixture burnt, and the backward thrust of the expelled gases pushes the plane forward. This engine was developed by two men working independently: Frank Whittle in England and Hans von Ohain in Germany in the 1930s.

Radio

*Guglielmo Marconi,
1874–1937*

Radio is a way of sending signals by electro-magnetic waves. Unlike other electrical communication systems—the telegraph and telephone —it does not use wires. Because of this it was first called *wireless*.

Electro-magnetic waves travel out from the sun through space to the earth. James Clerk Maxwell proved that they exist in 1864. These waves vary in length: some lengths we see as light, some feel as heat, and many others we are not normally aware of. (By wave-length scientists mean the distance from the crest of one wave to the next.) In 1888 Heinrich Hertz discovered wave-lengths which could be transmitted electrically and invented apparatus to produce them. In 1895 Marconi, an Italian, made a machine which could send and receive signals using Hertz's waves.

Marconi's radio was used as a telegraph to send signals at first. Other inventions turned it into the radio we know today. These inventions include Lodge's tuned circuit so that the receiver would pick up only the selected signal; Ambrose Fleming's valve (rather like an electric light bulb with a third wire sticking out) which impressed speech sounds onto the radio waves; Hughes' microphone which improved the quality of the sound; and many others. Marconi began experimental broadcasting in England in 1919, and the first broadcasting station was set up in the U.S.A. in 1920. Radio has many other uses, including navigation, plane landing and relaying information back from artificial satellites in space.

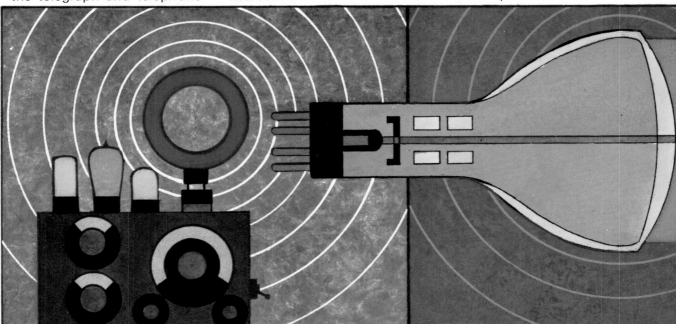

Television

Television uses electro-magnetic waves to send live and recorded pictures. A special camera changes the picture into an electrical pattern which is then changed back into a picture in the receiver (the TV set). Each second 25 to 30 new pictures are sent out, changed into electrical impulses, and then changed back into pictures. This produces a smooth and "continuous" moving picture because the human eye works too slowly to notice the breaks of vision between pictures.

The first successful television relay was made by Alexander Baird in Britain in 1926; but there were many problems to be solved before it was commercially possible, and regular television broadcasting did not begin until 1941 in the U.S.A. and 1946 in Britain.

As well as providing entertainment and news, television is used in long-range communication satellites. In 1959, Explorer 6 sent back the first TV picture of the earth. In 1961 Telstar was put into orbit to relay television signals across the Atlantic. Television has shown us men landing on the moon.

Television is also used in industry to watch processes where it is too dangerous or impossible for men to be: inside nuclear reactors, for example, or in flight tests to watch the operation of a plane's landing gear.

Artificial Materials

John W. Hyatt, 1837–1920

Artificial materials are made by chemically changing natural products or by combining simple chemicals. One of the first was Celluloid, made by an American, John W. Hyatt, from collodion, camphor and alcohol in 1868; the first films for the movies were made of it. In 1909 another American, L. H. Baekeland, made Bakelite, a non-flammable plastic. In 1938 the first purely *synthetic* fiber—nylon—was made from carbon, hydrogen, nitrogen and oxygen (the earlier rayons had been made from *natural* fiber). The range of such products is immense and increases almost daily.

The chemical industry made this development possible. From ordinary raw materials such as coal, oil, water, salt, limestone and sulfur, industrial chemists make the chemicals essential for the manufacture of every artificial product. The German Haber-Bosch process for making ammonia from nitrogen and hydrogen, for example, is the basis of a huge fertilizer industry, is used in refrigerators and air-conditioning units, and in the manufacture of dyes, drugs and fibers.

Rockets

The original rocket was a firework invented by the Chinese in about 1100 AD. It was made from a paper tube filled with gunpowder.

The rocket soon became a weapon, but it was not an important one until Germany made the V-2 bomb in 1944. This was a free-flight rocket: once ignited its flight path could not be changed. Rocket weapons now are guided missiles.

Wernher von Braun, 1912–

The V-2 rocket was propelled by liquid oxygen and an ethyl alcohol-water mixture; it had a 200-mile range and approached its target faster than the speed of sound. Both American and Russian artificial earth satellites and probes (see page 30) are launched with rockets developed from the V-2. Wernher von Braun, designer of the V-2, made the Saturn rocket used for Apollo spaceships.

When the explosive inside the rocket ignites, exhaust gases are expelled at the *back* creating the thrust that pushes the rocket *forward*. Because it does not use air as part of its fuel (as do jet and turboprop aircraft engines) the rocket can travel at great heights and in outer space. To achieve the great range necessary to launch a spaceship out of the earth's atmosphere, rockets have to be built in stages, which in turn ignite and fall away. Space flight would not be possible without the rocket.

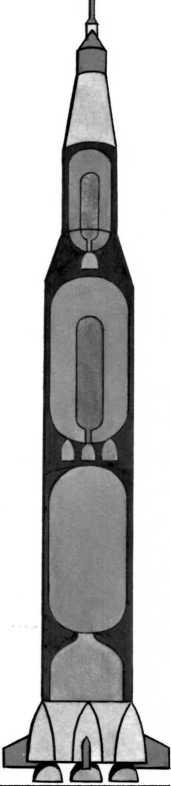

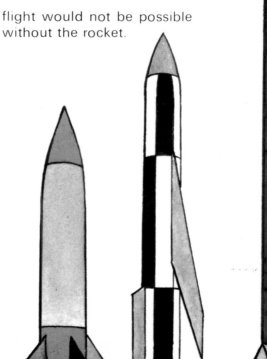

X-Rays

*Wilhelm Konrad Röntgen,
1845–1923*

X-rays are electro-magnetic waves—as are light, heat, and radio waves—produced naturally by the sun. They can also be made by passing high voltage electrical current through a tungsten filament in an airless tube: X-rays are given off as the fast moving electrons (particles of electricity) radiating from the filament are suddenly stopped by a tungsten rod at the end of the tube.

X-rays are very powerful and can pass through steel 11in. thick. They are normally invisible, but a beam of X-rays directed at a glass plate coated with zinc oxide will make it glow. If something is put between the X-ray machine and the plate, a light shadow will be cast. Doctors use X-rays to take internal pictures of the human body. Because bones are more dense than flesh, they will stand out more clearly in the picture; in this way doctors can see fractures and disease. Because X-rays destroy living cells they have to be used with great care; they are only used in large doses when doctors wish to destroy abnormal cells—such as cancer. X-rays are also used in industry to test metal joints and other structures.

X-rays were discovered in 1895 by a German scientist, Wilhelm Röntgen. He was experimenting with high voltage electrical current when he noticed that a screen painted with barium platinocyanide was lit up by some unknown source of radiation which he called X-rays. This was a most important discovery not only for medicine and industry but also for science, for X-rays have contributed to our understanding of the atom.

An atom, because it is the smallest amount of a chemical element that can enter into a chemical reaction, was thought to be indivisible. Physicists have proved that an atom subdivides further, that it has a nucleus around which electrons move at high speeds like planets in orbit round the sun. X-rays helped scientists locate the positions of electrons in atoms. X-ray crystallography (a method of crystal analysis) is an important research tool for exploring the structure of solids.

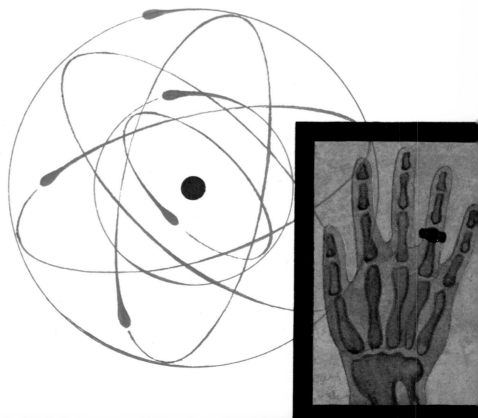

Nuclear Power

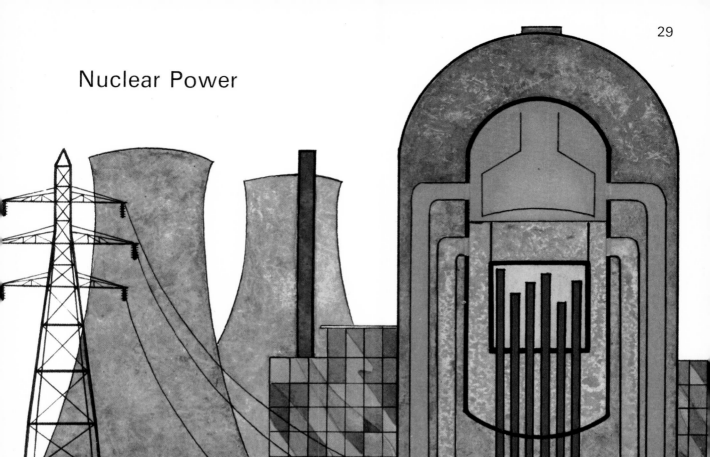

In 1919 the New Zealander Ernest Rutherford, who earlier had discovered the nucleus in the atom, split the nucleus of the nitrogen atom. Normally an atom is electrically neutral because the positive charge of the nucleus is balanced by the negative charge of the orbiting electrons: but if the nucleus is split this balance is upset and the energy of the nucleus released. When Otto Hahn split the nucleus of the uranium atom in 1938, a great deal of nuclear energy was released and scientists realized that this was an important new source of power. In 1942 in Chicago, Fermi produced a chain reaction from a uranium atom that led to the enormous power of the atom bomb.

To use nuclear energy for peaceful purposes the chain reaction has to be controlled in reactors. In America, Russia and England there are reactors in nuclear power stations providing electricity. In 1955 the American submarine *Nautilus* was the first to be run on nuclear energy.

This process of releasing nuclear energy by splitting the atom is called *fission*. The sun produces its energy by the opposite process—the *fusion*, or joining together, of two nuclei. The hydrogen bomb was made by nuclear fusion. But fusion is much harder to control than fission and scientists have still to make a satisfactory reactor. Fusion has two advantages over fission: it produces less harmful radioactive waste and because it can be produced

Otto Hahn, 1879–1968

artificially from deuterium, a heavy form of hydrogen and therefore available from water, it is virtually a limitless source of energy.

Space Exploration

Space exploration began with sounding rockets equipped with instruments to radio back information to tracking stations on earth. These rockets carried out, and still do, valuable scientific research.

The next stage was to put artificial satellites into earth orbit. Russia's Sputnik 1 was the first to be successfully launched in 1957. It circled the earth every 96 minutes at heights varying between 140 and 858 miles. America's first artificial satellite, Explorer 1, discovered the Van Allen Radiation Belt in 1958; in the same year Vanguard 1 sent back information establishing that the earth is pear-shaped. There are now in space artificial satellites that are traveling observatories with telescopes to observe the stars, weather stations to provide meteorological information, communication posts to relay telephone and television signals between Europe and America, and navigational stations to provide information to shipping.

Artificial satellites are launched vertically and then at a later stage tilted so that they are parallel with the earth. They remain in earth orbit unless designed to disintegrate. Before a manned satellite could be put into orbit tremendous problems had to be overcome: a craft had to be designed to protect the astronaut from extreme

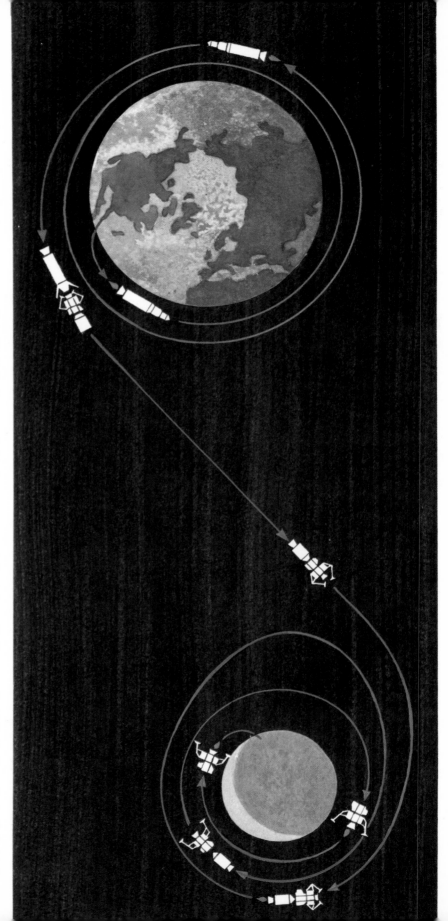

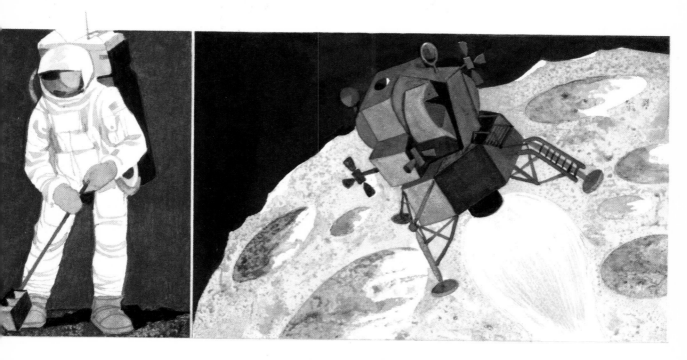

Neil Armstrong, 1930—

Edwin Aldrin, 1930—

Yuri Gagarin made the first manned space flight in Russia's Vostok 1 in 1961.

Spacecraft that escape the pull of the earth's gravity (and they must travel millions of miles to do so) are called probes. The first probes were unmanned: from them scientists have learned what the other side of the moon looks like, its temperature, and that its topsoil is rather like the earth's, making a soft landing possible. Probes have also mapped the surface of Mars and built up for us a working picture of outer space. In 1969 Neil Armstrong and Edwin Aldrin landed on the moon from Apollo 11's lunar module and then returned safely to earth.

heat and cold, pressure and radiation; it had to be equipped with oxygen breathing apparatus and insulated against the tremendous frictional heat of re-entry into the earth's atmosphere; and it had to be brought back safely to earth.

Underwater Exploration

Auguste Piccard, 1884–1962

Much underwater work and exploration is possible with suitable diving equipment. In a diving bell (a huge tank constructed so that air is trapped inside it) men can work underwater—laying bridge foundations, on dam constructions, in docks and harbors, etc. Equipped with breathing masks and air cylinders, free divers have made many important discoveries about marine life and conditions.

But this equipment is only suitable in relatively shallow water. To explore the ocean's depths (and echo-sounding apparatus, by sending electrical impulses to the ocean-bed, have measured depths of 36,000 ft.) equipment which protects the human body from the effects of pressure is essential.

The first such invention was William Beebe's bathysphere. It was a hollow steel sphere with port-holes for observation. In 1934 he dived 3,000 ft. in it. But it was attached by a suspension cable to a ship and this could not be made safe under certain wave conditions; should the cable break there was no way of recovering the bathysphere.

But the most important invention so far has been Auguste Piccard's free-diving bathyscaphe, or "ship of the deeps". This has a steel cabin equipped with its own air system; gasoline-filled buoyancy tanks, which when water is allowed in sink the craft; and iron shot ballast, which when released let the craft come to the surface. Piccard dived 10,000 ft. in the bathyscaphe in 1953, and his son Jacques 35,800 ft. in 1960.

From rock taken from the ocean-bed, scientists hope to find out how the earth, its continents and oceans originated.